THE ULTIMATE KEY TO UNLOCKING ONLINE RICHES

(MAKE YOUR DOLLARS ONLINE OVERNIGHT)

JD BIGWAMA

AMAZON KDP

ISBN-13: 9781234567890
ISBN-10: 1477123456

Cover design by: Art Painter
Library of Congress Control Number: 2018675309
Printed in the United States of America

DEDICATION

This book is dedicated to my wife Mrs. Anthonia Daniel who always prays for my success. I dedicate this book also to all the youth, especially the self-employed graduates all over the world who are with the thought of becoming employers rather than looking for employment, I pray our heart desires to be granted both now and always in Jesus' name amen.

INTRODUCTION

This book is inspired and written out of pure zeal to encourage and grow from rural and less privileged communities all over the world a society of millionaires, billionaires and even trillionaires in the next ten years. To achieve this goal the concept of multiplication must be our everyday formula i.e. every resources we have (especially time) is meant to be multiply and maximize because our maker's command is that of reproduction and multiplication to fill the available space- in my view that command is not only limited to human reproduction and multiplication but it includes multiplication of money, landed properties, and every resources we have. The digital age has brought about numerous opportunities for people to make money online. With the advent of social media, online marketplaces, and e-commerce platforms, anyone with an internet connection can start earning money from the comfort of their own home. Social media marketing, YouTube, affiliate marketing, online surveys, providing skillful services, online stores, tutoring, and crowdsourcing are just some of the ways people are making money online today. This forward aims to provide a comprehensive overview of each of these topics and how you can start making dollars from them.

Making Dollars from Social Media Marketing: Social media marketing is one of the most popular ways people are making money online. It involves promoting products or services on social media platforms like Facebook, Twitter, Instagram, and LinkedIn. This book will cover some effective techniques for social media marketing and how you can turn your social media presence into a profitable business.

YouTubing: The Most Effective Techniques for Social Media Marketing: YouTube is the largest video-sharing platform in the world, and it has become a significant source of income for many content creators. This forward will cover the most effective techniques for social media marketing on YouTube and how you can leverage the platform to make money.

Making Dollars from Affiliate Marketing: Affiliate marketing is a type of performance-based marketing where a person earns a commission for promoting someone else's products or services. This forward will provide an overview of affiliate marketing and how you can start making money from it.

Making Dollars from Online Survey: Online surveys are a quick and easy way to make money online. This forward will cover how online surveys work, which websites to use, and how you can maximize your earnings from them. Providing Skillful Services to Online Marketplaces to Earn Dollars: Online marketplaces like Fiverr and Upwork have made it easier than ever for people to offer their skills and services to a global audience. This forward will cover how you can leverage these platforms to provide skillful services and make money online.

Online Stores and How to Make Money from Them: E-commerce has revolutionized the way we buy and sell goods, and starting an online store has become an increasingly popular way to make money online. This forward will cover the basics of starting an online store and how you can make money from it.

Make Extra Dollars from Companies that Offer Online Tutoring: Online tutoring has become increasingly popular in recent years, and many companies are now offering opportunities for people to make money as online tutors. This forward will cover how online tutoring works and which companies offer opportunities to make extra dollars.

Crowdsourcing: A New Way to Make Money Online: Crowdsourcing is a way of outsourcing tasks or projects to a large, undefined group of people or community. This forward will cover the basics of crowdsourcing and how you can make money from it.

Conclusion: The internet has opened up numerous opportunities for people to make money online, and the topics covered in this forward are just a few of the many ways you can earn dollars from the comfort of your own home. Whether you're looking to supplement your income or start a full-time online business, these topics will provide you with the information and resources you need to get started.

TABLE OF CONTENTS

CHAPTER 1

MAKING MONEY FROM SOCIAL MEDIA MARKETING

Introduction: Social media marketing refers to the use of websites and social media platforms to promote a good or service. To accomplish marketing and branding objectives, it entails writing and publishing content on social media platforms. Social media marketing can encompass a variety of strategies, including creating and disseminating written, visual, and auditory material that engages the audience, running social media adverts, and interacting with people on social media platforms. Increasing brand recognition, generating website traffic, and ultimately boosting sales or other desired outcomes are the objectives of social media marketing for businesses or organizations. For starters it seems tough, anyway relax and have no problem because you can make it through the eight principled steps I am going to teach you here.

Eight principles of social media marketing

1. **Have a comprehensive knowledge of your audience**: Your success as a social media marketer comes from putting your audience as a top priority in your preparation to convince them. To have a comprehensive knowledge of your audiences means to ask fundamental questions like: (i) **who are my audience** (men/women, old/young, married/singles etc) (ii) **what easily get their attention** (games, movies, fashion, phone and other electronic gadgets, best food and drinks, etc) (iii) **where do they spend most of their time** (beer palor, restaurant, church, viewing centre, facebook, instagram, telegram,

whatsapp, snapchat, tiktok, Linkedin, etc). Having this understanding will give you an edge to create content in proportion to their gender, age, faith/belief system, fashion, interest, and lifestyle. Content must also fit in to their political, cultural or social affiliation: Most importantly you must when, where and how to approach them and make your content proposal.

2. **Identify what results you want from your audience**: Increasing brand exposure, generating leads, growing followers, engaging them in discussing your product, or website traffic are some of the most popular social media marketing objectives. Picking only one or two can help you stay focused and keep things simple. The most crucial thing to keep in mind while creating your goals is to make sure they are time-bound, relevant, detailed, quantifiable, attainable, and specific. You may improve the outcomes of your social media marketing by setting intelligent goals namely.

- **Decide on your metrics**: After you have set your objectives, you must be able to measure the outcome. Here are some of the popular social media marketing metrics:

(i) **Engagement rate**: The sum of the likes, shares, and comments divided by the total number of impressions for the content.

(ii) **Clicks**: The quantity of clicks on a specific post or piece of information.

(iii) **Reach**: The overall number of viewers of your post.

(iv) **Sentiment**: The emotion that your target audience experience when they view or engage with your content (good or negative). Make sure your metrics for measurement are closely related to your goals as you set them. For instance if your objective is to raise brand awareness, you must concentrate on gauging reach through impressions and shares

3. **Pick the appropriate channels**: Hypothetically I discovered that 74% of US people with a college degree

used Facebook, 85% use YouTube, 69% use Snapchat and 75% use Instagram. When choosing social media channels or platforms to promote your brand, consider choosing platforms where your target audiences are most likely to be found. Create your firm profiles on those platforms, or enhance the ones that already exist, once you've decided which ones to prioritize. Consistent branding across all platforms and current information about your brand should be present.

4. **Specify the most suitable content combination**: Here, examining your competitors' social media profiles can be a smart point to start. Even while originality and uniqueness are crucial for social media marketing, getting some ideas from others never hurts. The 80/20 guideline can help if you're unsure about what to post. This indicates that you should devote 80% of your content to entertaining, educating, and enlightening your audience. And 20% of your time should be devoted to formally advancing your brand. You can also get inspiration from the newest social media trends, including utilizing Stories as a content format, publishing material with a purpose of emphasizing diversity. Make sure to adopt a consistent theme, color scheme, style, and voice that reflect your brand identity regardless of the content kinds or formats you employ. As a result, your followers will know what to anticipate from you and have a motivation to interact with your content. Laying out your posts on social media management tools before publishing them is the best method to ensure you stick to a consistent theme (filters, captions, and creative touches). Before you actually publish your posts, tools like Preview, for instance, can help you get a sense of how they might appear in your feed.

5. **Construct a posting calendar**: You should upload material often and at the right moments to increase the return on investment from your social media marketing efforts. Post your material when it will most likely be seen

and interacted with by your target audience. Some social media management solutions include capabilities that can automatically optimize your post scheduling, which might help you decide when to post. Examining industry statistics could also be beneficial. The optimal days and times to publish on social networks differ based on your sector, according to analysis of numerous researches on post timings for social media. B2C businesses on Instagram gain by posting at 8am, 1pm, and 9pm. Meanwhile, at 9 a.m., 12 p.m., and 3 p.m., media organizations should post on Instagram. The optimal posting days can also change, but here is a brief breakdown: It's preferable to use social media management tools like Buffer, Sendible, or Agorapulse to automate your publishing depending on your social media calendar, regardless of what days and hours are convenient for you. With the help of these tools, you will be able to organize and schedule a number of posts in advance (together with appropriate captions and hashtags), eliminating the need for you to be present all the time.

6. **Focus on commitment**: The effectiveness of your social media marketing depends on promptly responding to your audience. You're leaving a lot of money on the table if you don't respond to their queries, remarks, or shoutouts right away. Ineffective audience engagement might cause you to lose followers and hurt the perception of your brand. On the other side, prompt responses can assist you in starting relevant discussions about your business and gaining respect and trust from others. Don't let a single query, comment, or mention go unanswered. You may track brand mentions with the aid of social listening platforms like Mention, Hootsuite, or Brandwatch to successfully communicate with your audiences.

7. **Analyze and improve**: Monitoring and evaluating your achievements should be the last phase in your social media plan. Check to identify which of your posts or marketing

initiates are bringing in the most visitors to your website or generating the most purchases. To make sure that your objectives are achieved, take a look at your success metrics and continuously modifying and redefining your plan as needed. You may improve your techniques to maximize profits by continuously testing to see what is and what is not working. If you're new to the world of social media marketing, it could seem like a lot, but try not to become overwhelmed. If you take the time to carefully follow each of the instructions in this tutorial, in little time you ought to be able to master the art of social media marketing!

Common terms used in social media marketing and their meanings

1) **Engagement**: The degree of communication and connection a brand has with its social media audience.
2) **Reach**: The total population that has viewed a specific social media post.
3) **Impressions**: The overall count of times a specific social media post has been seen.
4) **Hashtag:** A word or phrase that is used to group content and make it simple for other users to find. It is always preceded by the sign "#."
5) **Influencer**: A person with a sizable social media following who has the power to sway the thoughts and actions of their followers.
6) **Algorithm:** A system of rules and calculations determines what content is shown to visitors on social media platforms.
7) **Engagement rate**: The proportion of viewers who interact with a certain social media post or advertisement out of all the viewers.
8) **Organic reach**: The number of users who view a specific social media post or advertisement without any paid promotion or marketing.
9) **Paid reach**: The amount of individuals who view a specific social media post or advertisements as a consequence of paid

promotion or marketing

10) **Retargeting**: The act of displaying adverts to consumers who have already interacted with a business or gone to its website

11) **Referral traffic**: Refers to the number of visitors that a website gains from direct links rather than a search results page. Visitors from referral traffic typically find a website through direct links from another organization's webpages, also called backlinks.

12) **Click-Through Rate (CTR):** Refers to the percentage of users who click on a specific link that directs them to a website or landing page, out of the total number of people who view the link.

13) **Conversion**: Is the act of getting someone to take the action that you want them to take (e.g. click on your ad, subscribe to your email list, buy your product, etc.)

14) **Lead generation**: Is the process of converting potential customers into leads by persuading them to give you their email addresses.

15) **Analytics**: The measurement, collection, analysis, and reporting of data from social media platforms to inform marketing decisions.

Frequently asked questions on social media marketing and their attempted response:

1. What are the 5 P's of social media marketing? - They are: **product, price, promotion, place** and **people**. These are the essential framework that guides marketing strategies.

2. What are the 4 E's of social media marketing? – They are education, empowerment, entertain and engage. Each of them is a way of making your consumer fall in love with your product.

3. What are the 4 C's of social media marketing? – They are content, conversation, community and connection

4. What are the five core pillars of social media marketing?

– They are: Strategy, Planning and Publishing, Listening and Engagement, Analytics and Reporting, Advertising. According to Statista, the number of people worldwide who use social media increased from 3.6 billion in 2020

5. What is the most popular social media platform? - Statista shows that Facebook, YouTube, and WhatsApp are the leading social networks, with over two billion active social media users.

6. How long does the average person spend on social media per day? - According to a source, an average of 144 minutes daily was spent by internet users on social media and messengers, an increase of over 30 minutes since 2015; Latin America was found to have the highest average.

7. What is the fastest growing social media platform? - Data suggests that TikTok has seen an impressive 300 million growth in active users since January 2019, rising by 37.50%.

8. What's the best time to post on social media to reach my target audience? - Sprout Social data shows that most social media engagement occurs between 8 am and 2 pm on weekdays. It's also important to note that interaction significantly decreases outside those hours, before 4 am and after 8 pm daily.

9. How often should businesses post on social media? - Many studies and social media specialists suggest that posting to social media once daily is optimal, at most two daily posts.

10. How to measure the success of my social media strategy? – from the reaction on every post, when the number of followers increase, examine click-through rate, referral traffic, find out your reach,

11. Where should I direct my social media traffic? - Creating a website or blog is essential in effectively deploying digital marketing campaigns.

CHAPTER 2

YOUTUBING STEP BY STEP

Introduction: Youtube is defined simply as a website for sharing videos. Steve Chen, Chad Hurley, and Jawed Karim, three ex-workers of the American e-commerce firm PayPal registered it on February 14, 2005. The business's main office is in San Bruno, California. In May 2005, when the site was initially set up on a limited ("beta") basis, it started receiving about 30,000 visits every day. On December 15, 2005, YouTube made its formal launch, getting more than two million video views daily. By January 2006 the number increased to more than 25 million views per day. In March 2006, there were more than 25 million videos on the website, and each day, more than 20,000 new videos were added. YouTube served more than 100 million videos daily by the summer of 2006, and the rate of video uploads to the platform showed no signs of slowing down. Due to its rising expenditures couple with inability to monetize the website, founders started looking for who would purchase the website. Meanwhile a video service called Google Video was introduced by the American search engine business (Google Inc.) in 2005, but due to low traffic Google Inc. offered to acquire YouTube in November 2006 for $1.65 billion shares. Instead of merging their own video service with the acquired YouTube they continued running YouTube as it had been. Google struck agreements with a number of entertainment businesses to let copyrighted video content be uploaded on YouTube so that YouTube users would be legally permitted to include specific copyrighted songs in their videos upload on the website.

Why YouTube is the best tool for social media marketing

On YouTube, you have a tremendous opportunity to connect with your audience because almost everyone uses it for one reason or another. Statistically speaking YouTube has 2.6 billion monthly active users globally, almost 75% of Americans age 15years and above uses YouTube network thereby making it the second most widely used network next to Facebook and the second most popular website in the world next to Google. Straight from their Ads & Commerce Blog, Google states that 70% of viewers have bought from a brand after seeing it on YouTube. That shows just how efficient YouTube can be for driving conversions on products and services when used as a marketing tool. It is therefore needless and stressful to keep shouting on the roof top about your product while there is a useful and most productive tool to use with little or no effort and make your dollars in a jiffy.

Building a YouTube marketing strategy in ten steps

1. **Establish a YouTube channel:** To get a YouTube channel you must first register for a Google account since YouTube is a division of Google after which you sign up for the channel. There are two options to select from; namely you can either make use of any of your existing Google account or create a brand new account just for managing your business. The better option I know is to create a brand new account than using your personal Google account to manage your YouTube channel. One benefit of having a brand new account is that it allows your business to have numerous managers who can update and administer your YouTube channel; it will also keep separate and secrete your personal private life from public. Here I am going to teach you step by step how to create a YouTube channel hence pay attention and follow carefully.
    Step 1- You create a Google account: Presumably you already have a Google account with Gmail, Google Maps, or Google Play please skip and go straight to the next action. But if you're just getting started, find hereunder how to create a new Google

account.

Step 2- you create a YouTube account: Now that you have a personal YouTube account with your Google account you'll need to create a Brand Account if you want to use YouTube for your business. Enter a name for your Brand Account by going to your YouTube account page, clicking Create a Channel, and then clicking next. Giving various people admin access and customizing the name and style of your YouTube Brand Account will help it better represent your brand. It's interesting that YouTube gives you access to YouTube Analytics, which provides incredibly useful information about who is watching your videos and what content is most popular.

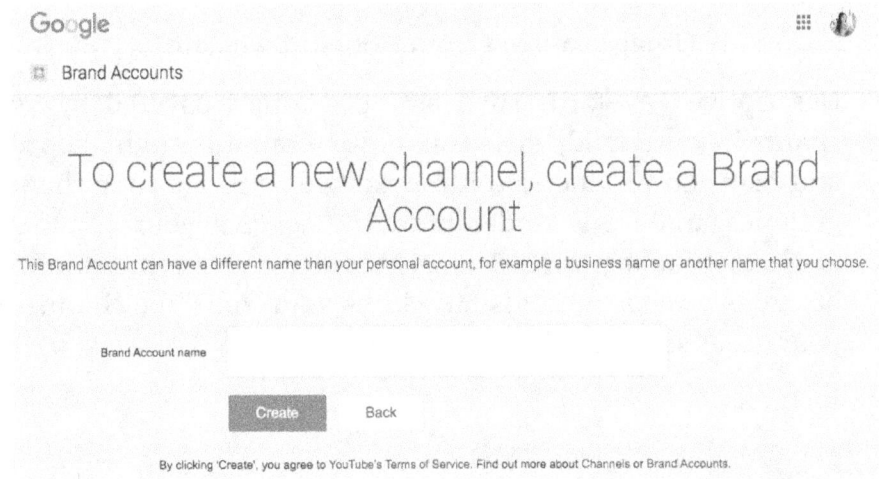

Step 3- you customize your YouTube channel: Choose Customize channel from the dashboard for your channel. Enter information to assist your channel to be more audience-discovery and friendly on the three tabs: Layout, Branding, and Basic Info. While filling out this information use descriptive keywords to help your account appear in searches.

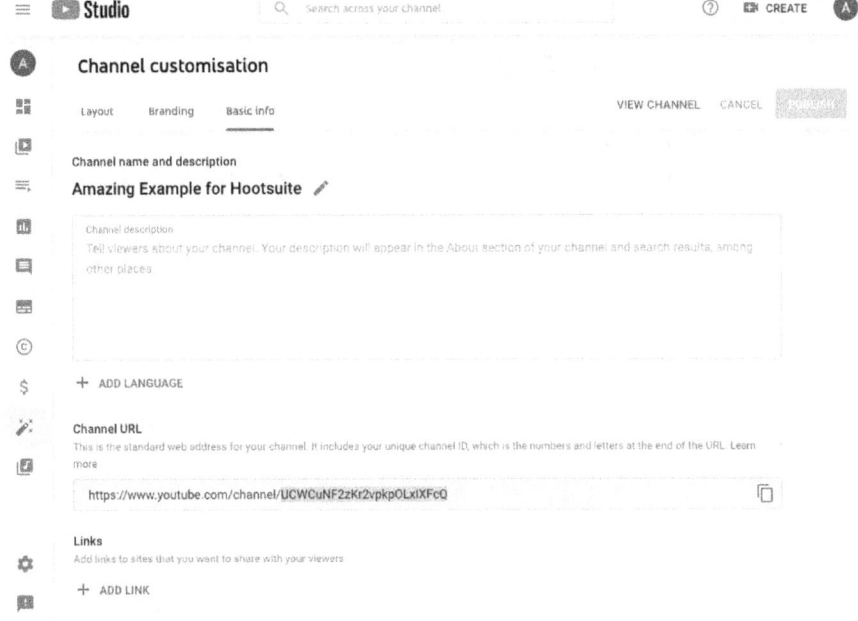

(Image sourced from Hootsuit website)

Descriptive keywords such as - the topics covered by your channel, your field, questions your content might address, and featured products. You may as well submit your channel graphics and icons under branding to give your channel a distinctive appearance. The appearance must represent your brand as a whole and visually links your YouTube channel to your other social media profiles and website.

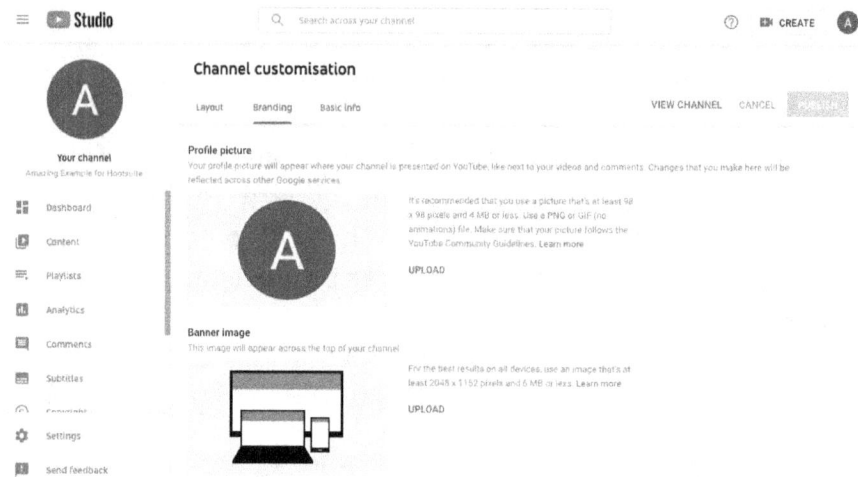

Step 4- you upload your first YouTube video: The Create button is located in the top-right corner click on it, and then follow the prompts to publish your first video.

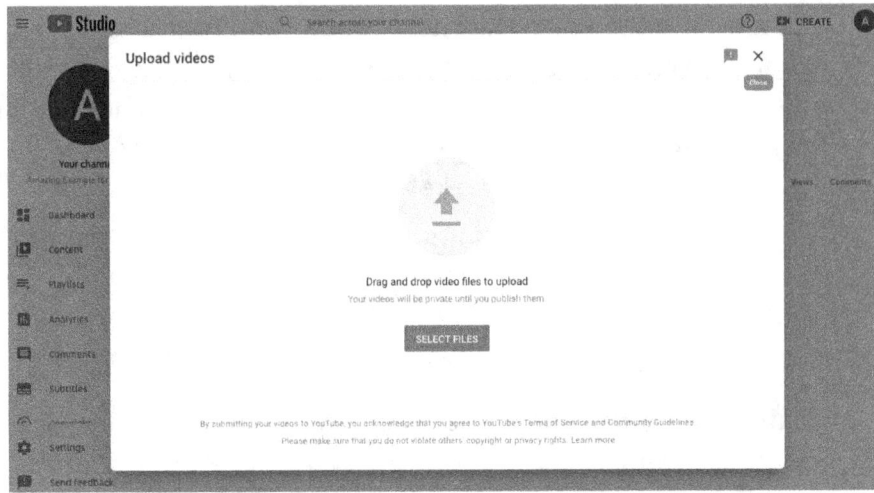

Step 5 - you make your YouTube channel discoverable: You should optimize your channel's content for discovery so as to increase views and subscriber counts. Other things you can do to enhance your channel popularity includes but not limited to: **optimizing video titles**- Users notice titles first, but they also aid search engines in determining the subject matter of your videos, **optimizing your YouTube description**- To make it easier for visitors to find what they're searching for, **create a "table of contents" with timestamps**, **add tags** - To find people who are really interested in content similar to yours, **include YouTube tags that are pertinent to your work**- YouTube algorithm can better understand your content when you use tags. To ensure that the search engine displays your videos to the appropriate audience, **add one or more categories, cross-promote** - To let your current admirers know you're launching a video empire, include a **link to your YouTube channel** and to your other social media profiles, website, and email signature, **use eye-catching channel art and thumbnails** - When a user is scanning search results, thumbnails help them pick what to watch. This implies that you must convey more than just the subject matter of your video, **choose a prefer channel icon** – channel icon is like a logo representing your YouTube presence hence it should match your brand

and compliment your channel banner, **create playlist, create a channel trailer, create great content consistently, schedule videos uploads, understand your audience, experiment with YouTube advertising** and **ask viewers to subscribe** etc.

2. Recognize your target market/audience

(i) What does your audience truly desire?

(ii) For whom are you producing videos?

(iii) What are they currently seeing on other YouTube channels?

According to a previous statement, YouTube has more than 2 billion subscribers, and 75% of internet users in the United States frequently visit the site. YouTube is used by 75% of those ages 15 and above, this is unlike other social media sites, the percentage of users doesn't significantly decline as people become older. Check out your Analytics page if you've already set up a YouTube channel. You will learn a lot about the characteristics and interests of your audience through this. You can determine how many people are coming across your videos via search, suggested feed, or other channels.

3. Analyze the competition in your target market

The quickest approach to gain subscribers on YouTube is to study what your competitors are doing that is successful. Analyze your competitors for the following: numbers of subscribers, average video views, frequency of posting, general ranking of the video, Observations made in the comments section, the principal subjects they discuss. To crown it all make a SWOT analysis using all the information gathered (SWOT stands for - strengths, weaknesses, opportunities, and threats) also contemplate these questions:

What are the most watched videos there?

What impression are they making?

What is the tone of their brand?

How can I set my business unique from theirs?

What suggestions for fresh content can I obtain from this channel?

After every findings you must do something better than your competitor.

4. Watch your preferred networks to learn

The networks you will learn from don't have to be focused on your field. You may discover a lot about what's effective by watching YouTube stuffs, especially given how frequently it changes. For instance, did you know that good audio quality is more crucial than good video quality? Yes poor audio can discourage viewers or subscribers from seeing your video. Making YouTube videos that viewers want to watch requires a lot of effort. Pay attention to the following when observing others: Thumbnails of videos, TV art, how other authors are linking to their articles or products, and how other makers alter their videos, using text popups and other extra effects. There are even entire channels that are devoted to YouTube expansion and video manipulation. You may monitor these, along with keywords pertaining to YouTube development.

5. Make your videos more compelling to attract viewers

Every day, YouTube's more than 2 billion viewers watch 1 billion hours of video content. How can you then get your clips to be seen by YouTube's algorithm by standing out from the competition? With one significant exception: Personalization, YouTube operates similarly to SEO and Google's algorithm. You often see the same webpage results when you conduct a Google search for a particular term. I say "approximately" since some findings vary by region. However, if you and a friend were seated next to each other in the same space, using the same Wi-Fi, and conducting the same search, you would get the same results. On YouTube however the story is not the same.

When YouTube displays search results, it takes into account the term and other factors like the popularity of the video and keywords in the title that Google looks for. But YouTube also takes into account your viewing history and the kinds of videos you typically watch. The YouTube homepage or search results of any two users won't be exactly the same. Personalization helps, but there are still other YouTube SEO tasks that must be completed if you want your videos to appear in search results. The following six methods can help you optimize your videos for increased viewership:

(a)   **Research keywords**: By conducting keyword research, you may learn the terms readers use to find content and incorporate them into your own. To conduct keyword research, use Google Keyword Planner. You can also enter your topic into the YouTube search bar to see what results appear. All of these queries were made by actual people. This may inspire you to think of new key phrases.

Your video should include your keywords.

For each video, you ought to include one core keyword as well as a few supplementary ones. You can include them here:

- The title (primary keyword) of the video
- The video description (primary keyword plus one or two related keywords
- In the opening three sentences, include the primary keyword.
- Tags of the video

(b)   **Utilize timestamps**: Timestamps on YouTube are similar to dividing your video into chapters. The areas they are most interested in can be skipped over by viewers. This raises the likelihood that they will view more of your video.

(c)   **Make a thorough explanation for the video**: A distinct segment of a few phrases detailing the subject matter of each video should be included in the description. However, you can establish default descriptions for the segments of each video that you want to see quickly. What you should put in your description is as follows:

- Web address

- Links to your other social networking accounts

- Links to the goods or services that you mention in the video

- An exhortation

(d) **Make a captivating thumbnail for the video**

Customized thumbnails are essential for views. The only other factor users often considered to decide as to whether or not watch your video is your title. Your target demographic will determine what makes a decent YouTube thumbnail. Don't just use a screenshot from your video, at the very least. To draw readers in, use a picture or aspects of your brand and some text.

(e)   **React to comments**

Is it true that YouTube is a social network? So behave accordingly. Responding to audience feedback demonstrates that your goal is community building rather than self-promotion of your own content. More comments result in a video that appears to be more popular and further raises its status in the algorithm.

6.   **Your videos should be uploaded and scheduled:** Your completed video can be directly uploaded into YouTube Studio, where you can choose to publish it now or at a later time. The same way you should schedule all of your other social media stuffs in this manner: How frequently will you post? Choose a timetable, such as daily, weekly, bimonthly, or monthly, and follow it succinctly. Consider the most effective day to post for your audience. When do people tend to watch your videos the most?

7. **Optimize your channel to attract viewers**: We've talked about optimizing individual videos but you also need to optimize

your entire channel. Make sure your channel art and profile photo reflect your branding. In addition to visual branding, YouTube has some built-in features that make it easier to get more subscribers:

- Group your videos into playlists organized by topic
- Create a channel trailer, which is like a commercial representing what your channel is about
- Ask people to subscribe to your channel and like, comment and/or share your video
- Have a clear call to action
- Engage with your audience in discussion

For example, mention how audience questions inspired the current video. Use a custom end screen to direct viewers to other videos of yours to keep them on your channel longer. Add closed captioning. You should prioritize accessibility in all your content, and captions include Deaf and/or hard-of-hearing people in your potential audience. Uploading your own captions will ensure accuracy and is something you can easily outsource. YouTube also offers free, automatic captioning but it often gets words wrong. You can even add translated versions of your captions to better serve a multilingual audience or earn more international views.

8. **Try YouTube advertising**: The majority of YouTube advertisements are videos, although banner ads can also be placed on the website or within videos. You can create your video advertisements with or without the ability to skip after, say, 5 seconds. Prior to engaging with paid advertisements, make sure you have the following: A firm grasp of who your audience is.

• Enhanced the visual branding and description of your YouTube channel.

• Post at least 5–10 videos so that potential customers may see what you're all about.

9.   **Try influencer marketing**: YouTube influencers also called "creators" are growing every year. YouTube reported a 50% year over year growth in the number of creators earning over $10,000 per year, and a 40% increase in those earning over $100,000. While new social platforms pop up all the time and become the "hot" place to advertise, like TikTok in 2021, YouTube is a high-performing channel for brands. Almost half of all brands who plan to use influencer marketing will use YouTube.

-      Choose an influencer who aligns with your brand and who you trust to produce high-quality content.
-      Analyze your results after the campaign and learn what to do differently next time. Nike's campaign with "What's Inside?" shows what's possible when you let your creator take the lead. Famous for cutting everyday items in half to see what's inside, the aptly-named channel created a series of videos for Nike to promote a new shoe. The most popular video of the series is where they cut the new shoe in half, which earned over 7.1 million views.

10. **Analyze and adapt**: As with all marketing, you need to track your YouTube analytics at least monthly. Use the built-in reports to see what your audiences are watching, what they like the most, where your traffic is coming from and more. Use analytics to track your channel growth, too. Write down your numbers monthly for:

- Subscribers
- Views
- View duration
- Top videos
- Watch time
- Impressions
- Your click-through rate (CTR)

This becomes your benchmark to measure your channel's growth rate each month. Not growing? Then it's time to adjust your

YouTube marketing strategy.

Frequently asked questions and answers

1. How can YouTube marketing benefit my business? A: YouTube marketing can help your business reach a wider audience, build brand awareness, and increase sales by providing a platform to showcase your products or services through engaging video content.

2. How do I create a YouTube channel for my business? A: To create a YouTube channel for your business, go to youtube.com and sign in with your Google account. Click on your profile picture and select "Create a channel." Follow the prompts to set up your channel and start uploading videos.

3. What types of videos should I create for my YouTube channel? A: You should create videos that showcase your products or services, provide valuable information to your audience, and engage them in a meaningful way.

4. How do I optimize my YouTube videos for search? A: To optimize your YouTube videos for search, include relevant keywords in your video title, description, and tags. Also, create high-quality, engaging video content that will encourage viewers to watch and engage with your videos.

5. How can I increase engagement on my YouTube videos? A: To increase engagement on your YouTube videos, encourage viewers to like, comment, and share your videos. Respond to comments and engage with your viewers to build a relationship and encourage loyalty.

6. How do I measure the success of my YouTube marketing efforts? A: To measure the success of your YouTube marketing efforts, track metrics such as views, watch time, engagement, and conversions. Use analytics tools such as YouTube Analytics to monitor your performance and make data-driven decisions.

7. How can I promote my YouTube videos to reach a wider audience? A: To promote your YouTube videos and reach a wider audience, you can share your videos on social media, collaborate with other YouTubers, run ads, and optimize your videos for search.

8. How can I monetize my YouTube channel? A: To monetize your YouTube channel, you can join the YouTube Partner Program and enable ads on your videos. You can also earn money through sponsorships, merchandise sales, and fan donations.

9. How often should I upload videos to my YouTube channel? A: You should upload videos to your YouTube channel on a consistent schedule, whether that's once a week, twice a month, or some other frequency that works for you and your audience.

10. How long should my YouTube videos be? A: The length of your YouTube videos will depend on the content and audience, but generally, videos between 3 and 10 minutes are most effective at engaging viewers and keeping their attention.

11. Should I create a YouTube channel if I don't have professional equipment? A: Yes, you can create a successful YouTube channel without professional equipment. As long as your videos provide value to your audience, they can be filmed on a smartphone or a basic camera.

12. How can I optimize my YouTube channel for conversions? A: To optimize your YouTube channel for conversions, include clear calls to action in your videos and descriptions, use annotations to encourage viewers to take action, and link to your website or landing pages in the description.

13. How can I use YouTube to build my brand? A: You can use YouTube to build your brand by creating high-quality, engaging videos that showcase your products or services, provide valuable information, and demonstrate your expertise in your industry.

14. How can I engage with my YouTube audience? A: To engage with your YouTube audience, respond to comments, ask for feedback and suggestions, run contests and giveaways, and create content that encourages interaction and participation.

CHAPTER 3

MAKING DOLLARS FROM AFFILIATE MARKETING

Introduction: Affiliate marketing is a contract between a merchant (also known as a "vendor," "store," "brand," or "someone selling something") and a publisher (also known as an "affiliate"), to whom the merchant pays a commission for traffic and/ or purchases created by their recommendations. According to Wikipedia, four important stakeholders are involved in this process are: the Advertisers, the Affiliates, the Affiliate platforms, and the **consumer**.

Advertisers: Also called enterprises, merchants, brands, vendors or sellers are the companies responsible for introducing products to e-commerce market hence crucial in the affiliate marketing process because without them the publishers would have no product to market. They are responsible for paying commissions to affiliates that drive traffic to their website.

Affiliates: Also known as publishers or partners are individuals or companies who refers a product to customers through internet advertising material and get paid in return for generating clicks, leads, and/or sales for advertisers. Acceptable means of advertisement includes emails, blogs, social media postings, forums, and other forms of publication. The publisher, like the merchant, is crucial to the affiliate marketing system

Affiliate platforms: Refers to the affiliate network which functions as a middleman, connecting the affiliate and the advertiser. When affiliates join the affiliate platform, they obtain access to advertiser's affiliate programs, likewise when advertisers join the affiliate platform; they gain access to affiliates that are ready to market their products for a commission. Generally the affiliate platforms provide contracting, tracking, reporting, and payment capabilities.

Consumers: The end users or potential customers and the most crucial component of the affiliate marketing system that click an affiliate's link. Consumers visit an advertiser's website and sign up or buy a product or service. The entire procedure makes more sense once you understand the major participants and their duties. Because there are financial incentives for everyone involved, it is in everyone's best interest to work hard and attract more consumers in order to convert more sales.

How does affiliate marketing work?

Let's break down affiliate marketing because it may be challenging to grasp at first. When a publisher or affiliate (partner) signs up for a brand's affiliate program, the brand gives them access to special tracking links. The affiliate then uses these links to promote the brand. The affiliate may include the links on its website, in social media profiles, email promotions, and other advertising venues. When customers click on these links, they are taken directly to the vendor's website where they can make purchases. For each purchase a customer makes, the brand pays the affiliate a commission.

How do affiliate commissions work?

Performance-based compensation is the norm in affiliate marketing. When certain "conversion events" occur, affiliates receive commission money. Any online user's action, like making a purchase of a product, the subscription to a newsletter, or the creation of an account, could be considered a conversion event. A selection of common payment schemes are typically used by the affiliate performance-based model, including:

1. Cost per action (CPA)
2. Cost per lead (CPL)

3. Cost per click (CPC)

What is an affiliate program?

A brand develops an affiliate program as a method or system to control affiliate marketing partnerships. Affiliates can participate in programs that brands design and oversee. Supporting the relationship between a brand and its affiliate partners is the objective. Contracts, payments, and sharing opportunities fall under this category. There are specific terms and restrictions for each affiliate program. An affiliate program includes three parties:

1. The affiliate
2. The brand or enterprise
3. The affiliate network/software as a service (SaaS) solution

Importance of High-Quality Traffic (HQT) in Affiliate Marketing Site

In the context of affiliate marketing, high-quality traffic aids in the achievement of your objectives and, if it converts (generates sales), then its quality. You'll need to make some adjustments if it doesn't convert. As you can expect, attracting high-quality visitors to your website is considerably more crucial than attracting untargeted readers. This is so that even if your overall traffic may be reduced when you concentrate on targeted visitors, your conversion rates will be higher. High-quality visitors might also benefit your website's search engine rankings. Readers who are specifically aimed at will be more inclined to share the material on your website and build links to it.

4 Principles Driving (HQT) to Your Affiliate Marketing Site

1. **Present High-Value Content**: You want your website's content to provoke thought and encourage action. In actuality, that is the fundamental definition of excellent content. High-value content is crucial if you want to increase visitors because it will be shared, discussed, and improve search engine rankings as a result. If you're prepared, use these instructions to make sure your

material is always valuable:

- **Respond to inquiries from your intended audience**: Utilize search engines to get answers to frequently asked queries in advance.
- **Include takeaways**: Give your reader a next move so they may start acting right now.
- **Cite statistics and examples from the real world**: To make your thesis clearer, give readers a taste of reality.

2. **Engage in social media activity**: Social media is a potent source of traffic that is incredibly targeted. After all, social networking sites like Pinterest, Instagram, and Twitter are essentially cloaked search engines. To help you get started, consider these suggestions:

4. **Set restrictions**: Target no more than three (or even just one or two) social media platforms at a time, as opposed to all of them. Narrowing your focus will help you achieve more fruitful outcomes.

5. **Decide on the best platform(s) for your sector**: Remember that each platform targets a distinct audience when choosing a platform (or platforms) for your specialty and make your decision appropriately.

6. **Maintain a regular posting schedule:** This will help you stay accountable and build a loyal audience.

7. **Try new things and track your progress**: By experimenting, you may find the best time and tone for your audience and so enhance your social media strategy.

Post as a Guest on Industry Blogs: Guest posting can be used as a tactic to increase the amount of high-quality visitors to your website. You might even use it to develop a specific audience. How can you increase your use of guest posts to promote your website? Here are a few things to remember:

8. **Write as a guest on blogs with a comparable audience**: Even if they're not as popular as other blogs, blog entries with a similar topic to your site will help you more successfully target your targeted audience.

9. **Integrate links into your article**. Include in the post links

to any of your own pertinent works.

Link Optimization on Your Site: You are aware of the value of links to your business because you are an affiliate. In other words, improving your links can increase their impact. Link cloaking and link shortening are both part of link optimization. You may do this to trademark your links and make them simple to post on social media. Luckily WordPress has plugins that let you carry out this action from within the platform.

How to get your affiliate link viral: As an affiliate your link which leads customers from your post on social media to the landing page of the advertises or to your personal blog/website and to the advertisers page in turn should always be incorporated in

10. Blog post
11. Coupon page
12. Product review
13. Banner advertisement
14. Product comparison portal
15. Email campaign
16. Social media channel

POPULAR AND HIGH REWARDING NICHES FOR AFFILIATE MARKETING

With the rise of e-Commerce, affiliate marketing is becoming an increasingly popular way to supplement one's income. It allows affiliates to earn money by referring customers to items, while businesses gain from the sales. According to one study, 63% of shoppers aged 18 to 34 trust influencers more than brand marketing when purchasing a product online. However, in order to develop a successful affiliate marketing program, you must first choose the greatest niche that distinguishes your company from the competitors. Thousands of affiliate offers are available in almost every niche. People are making thousands of dollars each month as passive income from this, and there is no reason why you can't too.

1. Click bank affiliate marketing
2. Amazon associate
3. Digistore 24
4. Alibaba affiliate marketing
5. Pinterest
6. eBay affiliate marketing etc

Here we will sample click bank affiliate marketing to talk further

There are a few things you can do to boost your success while you figure out how you want affiliate marketing to fit into your life:

- **Follow the ClickBank Blog**: Subscribe to the ClickBank Blog to receive weekly updates about affiliate marketing in your email. There is no greater method to achieve than to surround oneself with success information.

- **Join the ClickBank YouTube Channel**: The ClickBank YouTube Channel has a wealth of films designed to assist it's wealth of information that both entertains and instructs.

- **See the ClickBank Top Deals**. Check out these top ClickBank Offers if you're ready to get started right away.

- **Register for Spark**: Spark by ClickBank is our official affiliate marketing education platform, including courses, material, and a community to help you succeed as an affiliate marketer. Consider it an investment in your future and select a trustworthy, expert-curated, and gimmick-free source of information.

Frequently asked questions and their answers

1. What is affiliate marketing? Affiliate marketing is a type of performance-based marketing in which an affiliate earns a commission for promoting someone else's products or services.
2. How does affiliate marketing work? An affiliate promotes a

product or service to their audience and earns a commission for each sale or referral that they generate.

3. What are the benefits of affiliate marketing? The benefits of affiliate marketing include low start-up costs, the ability to work from anywhere, and the potential for high earnings.

4. How do I become an affiliate marketer? To become an affiliate marketer, you need to find a product or service that you want to promote, sign up for an affiliate program, and start promoting the product to your audience.

5. How do I find affiliate programs to join? You can find affiliate programs to join by searching online for products or services in your niche, or by reaching out to brands directly to inquire about their affiliate programs.

6. How much can I earn as an affiliate marketer? Your earnings as an affiliate marketer will depend on the commission rate offered by the product or service you are promoting, as well as the volume of sales or referrals that you generate.

7. What types of products or services can I promote as an affiliate marketer? You can promote a wide variety of products or services as an affiliate marketer, including physical products, digital products, software, courses, and more.

8. How do I promote the products or services I am affiliated with? You can promote the products or services you are affiliated with through your website, social media channels, email marketing, and other marketing channels.

9. Do I need a website to be an affiliate marketer? While having a website can be helpful for promoting affiliate products, it is not always necessary. You can also promote products through social media channels and other marketing channels.

10. What are some common affiliate marketing mistakes to avoid? Common affiliate marketing mistakes to avoid include promoting low-quality products, spamming your audience, and not disclosing your affiliate relationship with your audience.

11. Is affiliate marketing legal? Yes, affiliate marketing is legal as long as you comply with the guidelines and regulations set forth by the Federal Trade Commission (FTC).

12. How do I track my affiliate earnings? Most affiliate programs provide a dashboard or other reporting tools that allow you to track your earnings and performance metrics.

13. How do I get paid as an affiliate marketer? Affiliate marketers are typically paid through PayPal or other payment processors, or

through direct deposit to a bank account.

14. Can I be an affiliate marketer without a social media following? Yes, you can be an affiliate marketer without a social media following. However, having a strong social media following can help you reach a larger audience and potentially generate more sales.

15. How do I choose the right affiliate program for me? To choose the right affiliate program for you, consider the products or services you are interested in promoting, the commission rates offered, and the level of support provided by the affiliate program.

CHAPTER 4

MAKING DOLLARS FROM ONLINE SURVEY

Introduction: Companies that pay people to do internet surveys are known as paid survey companies. These enterprises often collaborate with companies, marketing agencies, and researchers who are looking for customer input and insights. In order to take part in a paid survey, you normally must sign up with the survey company and provide some basic demographic data. Using their demographics and interests, the survey company then matches participants with pertinent surveys. The length and complexity of the surveys can vary, but the average completion time is between 5 and 30 minutes. The means used by different paid survey organizations to remunerate workers vary; some provide cash payouts, gift cards, or other incentives. The length and complexity of the survey affect the payout amount as well.

Legitimate paid survey companies

1. **Swagbucks** - Swagbucks (https://www.swagbucks.com/) offers cash or gift cards as incentives for completing surveys, viewing movies, shopping, and other activities.
2. **Survey Junkie**: Survey Junkie (http://www.surveyjunkie.com/) provides cash incentives for completing surveys on a range of subjects.
3. **Vindale Research**: Vindale Research (http://www.vindale.com/) pays out in cash for completing surveys and writing product reviews.
4. **Toluna** - Toluna (http://www.toluna.com/) offers incentives for finishing surveys and taking part in online forums.

5. **Pinecone Research**: Pinecone Research () provides prizes in the form of cash or gift cards for completing surveys on a variety of subjects.
6. **MyPoints** – MyPoints (http://www.mypoints.com/) provides points for completing surveys, shopping, and other activities that may be exchanged for gift cards.
7. **InboxDollars** – With InboxDollars (http://www.inboxdollars.com/) you can earn money for completing surveys, reading emails, watching movies, and more.
8. **Harris Poll Online**- rewards users with points that can be exchanged for gift cards for completing surveys on a variety of topics.
9. **Branded Surveys**: Branded Surveys (https://surveys.gobranded.com/) provides points for completing surveys that can be exchanged for money or gift cards.
10. **YouGov** - YouGov (https://www.yougov.com/) provides points for conducting surveys on a variety of topics that may be exchanged for cash or gift cards.
11. **American Consumer Opinion**- https://www.acop.com

Five top ranking paid survey companies discussed

SWAGBUCKS

Since its establishment in 2008, Swagbucks has grown to become one of the most well-known rewards portals on the internet. The company provides a variety of free ways to earn SB points, including signing up for offers, completing surveys, and referring friends. Users of the Swagbucks website and mobile app get rewarded for participating in online activities like surveys, video watching, and online purchasing. Users collect "Swagbucks," or SB points, which may be exchanged for gift cards or cash back from well-known retailers including Amazon, Walmart, and Target. Swagbucks pays you in real money. One dollar in cash or gift cards is equivalent to 100 SB. Your gains can be exchanged for Amazon gift cards, gift cards from other well-known merchants, PayPal cash, prepaid Visa cards, or even a cheque in the mail.

STEP BY STEP SIGN UP

1. To sign up, go to https://www.swagbucks.com/ and click the "Sign Up" button in the top right corner. Finish the registration process by entering your information.
2. Finish your profile: Make sure your profile is finished before you start earning SB. This will help Swagbucks connect you with offers and surveys that are relevant to you. You will receive 2 SB just only completing your profile.
3. Browse the website: After signing up, take some time to browse the website and familiarize yourself with the different methods you can earn Swagbucks (SB). By taking surveys, viewing movies, purchasing online, completing offers, and engaging in other activities, you can earn SB.
4. Start earning SB: There are many different methods to do this on Swagbucks. The most well-liked techniques include watching movies, participating in polls, and purchasing online. You will receive a specific number of SB for each activity.
5. Redeem your SB: When you've gathered enough SB, you may trade them in for gift cards to well-known stores like Amazon, Walmart, and Starbucks. Additionally, you can use PayPal to convert your SB into cash.
6. You can earn money with Swagbucks' referral program by referring friends. If you invite your friends to join, you'll be paid a portion of their lifetime profits.

Survey Junkie

An online survey company called Survey Junkie pays participants with cash for completing questionnaires on various subjects. The business was established in 2013 and has since expanded to become one of the most well-known online survey providers. With easy-to-follow instructions and straightforward surveys, Survey Junkie provides a straightforward and user-friendly platform. The business pays customers with points that can be exchanged for cash via PayPal or gift cards to well-known stores like Amazon and Target. With some surveys giving up to $50 in incentives, the amount of payment varies based on the length and intricacy of the survey.

Pinecone Reasearch

Pinecone Research is regarded as one of the most exclusive survey panels due to its high-paying surveys and careful hiring procedures. Worldwide market research firm Nielsen owns and runs Pinecone Research, an online survey panel. You must receive an invitation from an existing member or through an affiliate link in order to join Pinecone Research. Once you're approved, you can begin taking surveys and earning points that may be exchanged for money or gifts. Surveys typically pay $3 and take 15 to 20 minutes to complete. Pinecone Research has a distinctive feature in that they occasionally send people tangible goods to test and provide feedback on. This can range from food and drinks to cosmetics and home goods. Users of Pinecone Research are paid via PayPal or cheque. With a $3 minimum payout requirement, it's simple to withdraw your money right away.

Generally speaking, Pinecone Research is a reliable and trustworthy survey panel that might be a fantastic choice for anyone wishing to work from home. Use this website link to know more about this great company https://join.pineconeresearch.com/

YouGov

A global market research and data analytics company called YouGov focuses on collecting and interpreting information from surveys of public opinion, social media, and other sources. Since its establishment in the UK in 2000, the business has grown to operate in more than 50 nations.

The major offering from YouGov is its online survey platform, which enables users to take part in market research surveys and receive incentives for doing so. Using its extensive database of consumer insights, the company also offers specialized research services to corporations and organizations, offering data-driven insights and suggestions. YouGov is renowned for its political polling, which has been used by news organizations and political campaigns all around the world in addition to its research and data analysis services. The business has also drawn interest for its "BrandIndex" tool, which tracks changes in customer perception of brands.

How to become a surveyor at YouGov

1. Meet the minimal requirements: You must possess a high school graduation or its equivalent, as well as some prior computer and internet technology working knowledge. You can also be asked to prove your ability to communicate verbally and in writing.

2. Apply for a job as a surveyor: On websites like Indeed and YouGov, you may do a job search for vacant openings. Send in your application, which can include a résumé and cover letter, and be ready to respond to inquiries about your qualifications and background during the screening process.

3. Complete a test for qualification: If your application is accepted, you will be required to take a qualifying test that evaluates your reading and comprehension skills, accuracy, and attention to detail.

4. Complete training: After passing the qualification test, you must complete training on the policies and practices of the organization as well as the technical aspects of conducting surveys on the YouGov platform.

5. Start conducting surveys: Once you've finished your training, you'll be able to do so on the YouGov platform. You'll get access to a dashboard where you may browse the surveys that are accessible and decide which ones to complete. By completing surveys, you will receive incentives that may be exchanged for money or other goodies.

Payment plan and withdrawal method at YouGov

Payment Plan:

1. Earnings: YouGov gives points to users who complete surveys; each point is worth a particular amount of money. The length and difficulty of the survey will determine how much money you can make by completing it.
2. Points: When you reach a specific threshold, you can exchange your points for a variety of incentives, including gift cards, prepaid debit cards, and PayPal cash.

Withdrawal procedure:

3. Gift Cards: YouGov offers a selection of gift cards from well-known merchants like Amazon, Walmart, and Best Buy. YouGov also provides prepaid debit cards, which may be used to make purchases and withdraw cash from ATMs much like regular debit cards.
4. PayPal: Your earnings can also be transferred right to your PayPal account.
5. Bank Transfer: YouGov provides bank transfer as a withdrawal option in various nations.

The payment schedule and withdrawal method may differ by country, so it's advisable to check the YouGov website for details unique to your area. Additionally, there can be costs connected with specific withdrawal methods, and some withdrawal methods might have minimum withdrawal amounts.

To join up for YouGov surveys, do the following:

1. Visit the YouGov website at https://www.yougov.com/
2. The "Join now" button is located in the top right corner of the website. Your name, email address, and birthdate are required fields on the registration form.
3. Pick a password, then confirm it.
4. At the bottom of the page, select "Join now."
5. A YouGov confirmation email should be in your inbox.
6. To verify your account
7. click the link in the email.

You can access the YouGov website and begin doing surveys when you have verified your account.

Branded Surveys

An online market research firm called Branded Surveys gives people the chance to take part in paid surveys and get rewarded for their insights. The company was established in 2012, and its main office is in San Diego, California. You must first register for a Branded Surveys account on their website and enter some personal details, such as your age, gender, and location. You will have access to a number of surveys that fit your interests and demographic profile once you have finished the basic registration process. You will receive points for each survey you complete, which may then be exchanged for gifts like gift cards, PayPal cash, and items. The number of points you receive for each survey will vary according to its length, complexity, and the amount of reward being provided by the research company. Additionally, Branded Surveys provides a referral program that enables you to gain extra points by recruiting loved ones to use the service.

Branded surveys are generally a good method to get paid or receive rewards for giving your opinion on a variety of subjects. Be aware that there are numerous survey websites available, so it's crucial to investigate and compare various platforms to determine which one best suits your interests and requirements. It's also crucial to remember that even though some surveys pay significantly; they might also take longer to finish or have particular qualifying conditions.

Frequently asked questions and answers

1. What are paid surveys? Paid surveys are questionnaires or polls conducted by companies or organizations to gather feedback or opinions from consumers in exchange for compensation.
2. How do paid surveys work? Companies or organizations create surveys and distribute them to panelists who have signed up to take surveys in exchange for compensation. The panelists complete the surveys and receive payment for their time and opinions.

3. How do I find paid survey opportunities? You can find paid survey opportunities by searching online for survey sites or by signing up for survey panels through market research companies.

4. How much can I earn from taking paid surveys? Earnings from paid surveys vary, but most surveys pay anywhere from a few cents to a few dollars per survey completed.

5. What are the payment methods for taking paid surveys? Payment methods for taking paid surveys include cash, gift cards, and other forms of compensation such as products or services.

6. Are paid surveys legitimate? Yes, paid surveys are legitimate as long as you sign up with reputable survey sites or panels.

7. Can I make a living taking paid surveys? It is unlikely that you can make a living taking paid surveys alone, as the pay is typically low and the number of available surveys may be limited.

8. What types of surveys can I expect to take? You can expect to take surveys on a wide range of topics, such as products, services, advertising, and current events.

9. How long do paid surveys take to complete? The length of paid surveys varies, but most surveys take anywhere from a few minutes to half an hour to complete.

10. Do I need any special skills or qualifications to take paid surveys? No special skills or qualifications are required to take paid surveys, but having knowledge or experience in a particular field may be helpful for some surveys.

11. Can I take paid surveys on my mobile device? Yes, many survey sites and panels offer mobile-optimized surveys that can be completed on a mobile device.

12. Can I take paid surveys from anywhere in the world? Paid survey opportunities may be limited to certain countries or regions, so it is important to check the eligibility requirements before signing up.

13. How often will I receive paid survey invitations? The frequency of paid survey invitations varies, but most panelists can expect to receive several invitations per week or month.

14. Are there any risks associated with taking paid surveys? There are some risks associated with taking paid surveys, such as providing personal information to unscrupulous survey sites or being scammed by illegitimate survey sites.

15. Are paid surveys a good way to make money? While paid surveys may not be a reliable source of income, they can be a good way to earn extra cash or gift cards in your spare time.

PART B: SELLING YOUR SKILLS ONLINE FOR A PAY

CHAPTER 5

PROVIDING SKILLFUL SERVICES TO ONLINE MARKET PLACES TO EARN DOLLARS

FIVERR

"Fiverr is a global online marketplace (world's largest freelancing website) that offers jobs and services, known as 'gigs,' starting at $5 per job accomplished, thus the name." The site is largely utilized by freelancers who use Fiverr to offer a range of services, as well as clients who purchase such services. Currently, Fiverr advertises over three million services ranging from $5 to $500 on the site."

Fiverr is made up of three parties:

The first is the website's founder, who is also its owner. I don't want to belabor the point, but these men make a lot of money doing practically nothing. They receive 20% of every transaction that goes via Fiverr. This means that if you sell a $5 gig, Fiverr keeps $1 while you keep $4. If 1 million transactions occur each day, these lads will earn $1 million dollars. The second party is YOU, who provide services on their platform, and the third party is the customer, who puts money into the system by purchasing your services. Any service you create on Fiverr will be priced at $5 by default.

FREELANCE

What is freelancing?

Freelancing is the practice of working as a self-employed individual who provides services to clients on a project-by-project basis as opposed to being hired full- or part-time by a company or organization. Typically working from home, freelancers are in charge of overseeing their own workload, budget, and customer connections. In a nutshell, freelancing is a form of self-employment where people provide their talents or services to clients on a contract basis. This can cover a wide range of professions, including those in writing, design, programming, marketing, and other fields. According to a recent freelancing research study by Upwork, more than one-third of the American workforce today is freelancers in some form.

Categories of freelancers

1. Freelancers in the creative industries: These are people who provide services including graphic design, writing, illustration, photography, and video production.
2. Freelancers who provide technical services: Services such as web development, software development, IT assistance, and data analysis, fall under this category.
3. Freelancers in marketing and PR: These are people who provide services in social media, content production, public relations, and marketing.
4. Freelancers in business and finance: These are those who provide services in the fields of project management, accounting, law, and finance.
5. Freelancers who provide consulting services: They include those who work in the fields of management, strategy, human resources, and training.
6. Personal service freelancers: These are those who provide personalized services including coaching, counseling, and personal training.
7. Hospitality professionals: Are freelancers who provide services like catering, hospitality, and event planning.

These are but a few of the numerous subcategories of independent contractors. The categories may overlap, and some independent contractors may provide services across several categories.

Practical freelancing industries

1. Writing and editing: Independent writers and editors can provide their services to clients in sectors like publishing, marketing, advertising, and journalism.
2. Graphic designers: Web design, branding, and advertising are just a few of the sectors where freelance graphic designers might find clients.
3. Web development: Contractors in the e-commerce, educational, and technological sectors can provide their clients with their services.
4. Photography: Clients in the fashion, advertising, and event planning sectors can hire freelance photographers to take their pictures.
5. Social media management: Independent social media managers can work with clients in e-commerce, marketing, and public relations.
6. Consulting: Clients in the managerial, financial, and technological sectors might use the services of independent consultants.
7. Translation: Clients in the publishing, legal, and medical sectors might use the services of freelance translators.
8. Video production: Independent video producers can work with clients in the entertainment, education, and advertising sectors.
9. Freelance virtual assistants: Can provide their services to clients in a range of businesses, providing assistance with administrative chores, customer support, and more.

There are many more freelancing industries, and these are but a few examples. For people who are skilled and knowledgeable in a certain field and wish to provide their services to clients on a flexible basis, freelancing might be a fantastic choice.

Steps to become a freelancer

1. Determine your abilities: Identify the talents, passions,

and interests you may provide to clients as services. This could include writing, graphic design, web development, social media marketing, and many other abilities.

2. Create a portfolio: Make a portfolio to display your abilities and examples of your work. Case studies, examples of previous accomplishments, and client recommendations are some instances of this.

3. Establish your pricing: Choose your hourly fee or project-based pricing depending on the services you provide, your experience, and the norms in the sector.

4. Organize your company: Set up your accounting system, register your business, and acquire any necessary licenses.

5. Develop your web presence: Make a website and social media presence that highlight your abilities and offerings. Utilize them to network and establish connections with prospective

6. Start looking for customers: Utilize social media, networking events, and online job boards to discover clients. You can also get in touch with potential customers directly and pitch your services.

7. Offer high-quality work: Once you've secured a client, stay in constant communication with them and offer high-quality work.

8. Ask for feedback: This necessary in order to build your portfolio and improve your services.

9. Producing high-quality work: To expand your firm, keep attracting clients by delivering quality work.

Keep in mind that it takes time, work, and persistence to succeed as a freelancer. To establish a solid reputation in your field, it's critical to maintain order, keep track of your cash, and constantly upgrade your abilities and offerings.

Popular freelance websites to apply for a job

1. Upwork: With more than 12 million clients and freelancers from all around the world, this is one of the biggest

freelance marketplaces. Through the site, freelancers may set up a profile, submit applications for contracts, and manage their work and payments.

2. Freelancer.com: This website offers a variety of freelance projects, including writing, marketing, and web development and design. In order to win work, freelancers might bid on projects and compete with one another.

3. Fiverr: Fiverr is a website where freelancers may list their skills in a variety of categories for as little as $5 per assignment. Freelancers can set up a profile, list their services, and wait for orders from clients.

4. Guru: This website provides a variety of freelancing opportunities in fields like web development, design, and writing. Through the site, freelancers may set up a profile, submit bids for jobs, and manage their work and payments.

5. Toptal: Toptal is a platform that links elite freelancers with excellent clients. Only the best 3% of independent contractors are accepted by Toptal after a strict screening process.

6. PeoplePerHour: This website provides a range of freelancing opportunities in industries like web development, design, and writing. Through the site, freelancers may set up a profile, submit bids for jobs, and manage their work and payments.

There are a plethora of other well-known freelance websites to pick from; these are but a few examples. It's critical to investigate and compare many platforms to choose which one best suits your expertise, field, and working style.

Three most popular freelance websites

1. Upwork - Upwork is the largest freelancing platform, with more than 18 million freelancers and more than 5 million clients enrolled.

2. Freelancer.com - One of the biggest platforms for freelancing, Freelancer.com has over 50 million registered

users, including freelancers and clients.

3. Fiverr - One of the most well-known freelance websites, Fiverr has more than 3 million active freelancers and more than 2 million registered buyers.

Reasons Upwork, Freelancer.con and Fiverr are the three most populous website for freelancing

1. Wide Range of Services: All three platforms provide a variety of services in a number of different fields, including writing, graphic design, programming, and administrative work. Clients can locate the best people for their project, while freelancers can find work in their particular field.

2. User friendliness interface: Each platform provides a user-friendly interface that streamlines the process of recruiting freelancers and finding employment. The platforms enable independent contractors each to set up a profile and present their qualifications. Similar to employers, clients can submit jobs and search freelancer profiles to find the best match.

3. Payment Protection: To ensure secure and open payments, all three platforms provide payment protection to clients and freelancers. Clients are safeguarded from frauds and subpar work because freelancers are only paid after the work is finished to the client's satisfaction.

4. Global Reach: These platforms are accessible to users all over the world, making it possible for customers and independent contractors to collaborate. This has made it simpler for companies to discover talent at an affordable price and for independent contractors to find employment from any location in the world.

5. Huge User population: These platforms have amassed a sizable user population over time, drawing millions of clients and freelancers. More users are now using the platforms to take advantage of the opportunities generated by this, creating a network effect.

Important factors to consider for evaluating the best freelance platform to join

1. User base: Consider the volume and diversity of platform users. Different platforms have different user bases, and some could be more well-liked in particular sectors or geographical areas.
2. Fees and commissions: Some platforms levied fees or took a cut of the freelancers' revenue. To find out how much you are can anticipate to make, look at each platform's costs and commission structure.
3. Payment protection: To make sure that freelancers are paid for their job, certain platforms provide payment protection or escrow services. To find out how secure your payments will be, look at each platform's payment protection policy.
4. Job availability: Consider the kind and amount of vacancies on the site. In some industries or localities, there may be more jobs on particular platforms, while on others, there may be greater competition for jobs.
5. Client quality: Consider the platform's clientele's profile and good standing. Different platforms could draw consumers of a better caliber than others, while others might have more difficult customers to manage.
6. User interface and tools: Take a close look at the platform's user interface and the tools offered to independent contractors. Other platforms could be simpler to use than others, and others might have more effective capabilities for client communication and project management.
7. Customer support: Consider the platform's level of customer support. Some platforms might provide more resources to assist freelancers than others do, and some might provide greater support than others.
8. When comparing various freelance websites, take into account these aspects as well as any others that are significant to you. You may uncover the best chances and establish a lucrative freelancing job by doing your

homework and picking the correct platform.

Web addresses for independent contractors

1. Upwork - http://www.upwork.com/
2. Freelancer.com - https://www.freelancer.com/
3. Fiverr - https://www.fiverr.com/
4. Toptal - http://www.toptal.com/
5. Guru - http://www.guru.com/
6. PeoplePerHour - http://www.peopleperhour.com/
7. Simply Hired, available at https://www.simplyhired.com/
8. 99designs - http://99designs.com/
9. Designhill - http://www.designhill.com/
10. TaskRabbit - http://www.taskrabbit.com/

The above additional websites are provided to help you search for more opportunities.

Frequently asked questions and answers

1. What is Fiverr? Fiverr is an online marketplace that connects freelancers with clients looking for services such as graphic design, writing, and programming.
2. How does Fiverr work? Freelancers can create a profile on Fiverr and offer their services to clients, who can then browse and purchase services based on their needs.
3. How do I get started as a freelancer on Fiverr? To get started as a freelancer on Fiverr, you need to create a profile, list your skills and services, and set your pricing.
4. How do I find clients on Fiverr? Clients can find your services through Fiverr's search engine or by browsing the Fiverr marketplace. You can also promote your services through social media and other marketing channels.
5. How does payment work on Fiverr? Payment is handled through Fiverr's platform, with clients paying upfront for services. Fiverr takes a commission on each transaction.
6. What are some best practices for freelancers on Fiverr? Some best practices for freelancers on Fiverr include delivering high-quality

work, communicating clearly with clients, and building a strong reputation through positive reviews.

7.   What are some common freelance services offered on Fiverr? Common freelance services offered on Fiverr include graphic design, writing, programming, social media marketing, and virtual assistance.

8.   What are some benefits of freelancing? Benefits of freelancing include the ability to work from anywhere, flexible schedules, and the potential to earn more money than in a traditional job.

9.   What are some challenges of freelancing? Challenges of freelancing include the need to constantly find new clients, managing your own workload and finances, and dealing with irregular income.

10. How can I set my prices as a freelancer on Fiverr? You can set your prices based on factors such as the complexity of the work, your experience and skill level, and the market rates for similar services.

11. How can I stand out as a freelancer on Fiverr? You can stand out as a freelancer on Fiverr by offering high-quality work, delivering on time, communicating well with clients, and building a strong portfolio and reputation.

12.   What are some common mistakes made by freelancers on Fiverr? Common mistakes made by freelancers on Fiverr include undercharging for their services, failing to communicate effectively with clients, and delivering low-quality work.

13.   How can I build a successful freelance career? To build a successful freelance career, you should focus on delivering high-quality work, building a strong reputation through positive reviews and testimonials, and consistently marketing your services.

14. What are some tools and resources for freelancers on Fiverr? Tools and resources for freelancers on Fiverr include project management tools, invoicing software, and freelance job boards and communities.

15. What are some tips for managing your time as a freelancer? Some tips for managing your time as a freelancer include setting clear work hours, prioritizing your workload, and taking breaks to avoid burnout

CHAPTER 6

ONLINE STORES AND HOW TO MAKE MONEY FROM THEM

Amazon:

In 1994, Jeff Bezos founded Amazon, an international technology company. The company started out as an online bookstore but has since grown to become one of the biggest e-commerce businesses in the world, providing a wide range of goods and services. In the beginning, Jeff Bezos ran Amazon out of his garage in Bellevue, Washington. The corporation was originally called Cadabra, but Bezos changed it to Amazon to honor the largest river in the world, which is located in South America. The name change reflected the company's goal of becoming the biggest bookseller in the world. In 1995, Amazon launched its website and started selling millions of books to customers all over the world. The company attracted devoted customers by providing excellent customer service, reasonable pricing, and timely delivery. With time, Amazon's product selection has expanded to include music, technology, clothing, and other goods. In 2002, the corporation launched Amazon Web Services (AWS), a cloud computing platform that has since grown to be one of its most lucrative divisions. With the launch of services like Amazon Prime, Amazon Fresh, Amazon Go, and numerous others, Amazon has continued to develop and innovate. With a market value of more than $1.5 trillion and more than one million employees worldwide, Amazon is currently one of the biggest organizations in the world.

Amazon's goods and services

It would be hard to enumerate all of the services that Amazon provides. Some of the most well-known Amazon services are listed below:

1. Online shop: When Amazon first started up, it sold a variety of goods online, including books, electronics, apparel, and more.
2. Amazon Prime: Members of this membership program have access to streaming music, TV shows, and movies, as well as free and speedy shipping on qualified orders.
3. The cloud computing platform Amazon Web Services (AWS) provides a range of services, including database management, computing and storage.
4. Amazon Advertising provides companies with the resources they need to create and publish adverts on Amazon's website and other platforms.
5. Amazon Marketplace is an online storefront where third parties can sell their products to Amazon customers directly.
6. Fresh vegetables, dairy, meat, and other products are available through Amazon Fresh, a grocery delivery and pickup service.
7. Amazon Go is a chain of stores that doesn't require customers to wait in line at the register or use cash registers by using cutting-edge technology.
8. Amazon Books: This is a chain of bookstores that offers both digital and physical books, as well as Amazon devices.
9. You can access millions of songs, playlists, and podcasts with Amazon Music, a streaming service.
10. Original television shows, films, and other content are available on Amazon Prime Video, a streaming platform.
11. In addition, Amazon provides a wide range of extra services, including Kindle, Fire TV, Alexa and many more.

Methods for earning on amazon

1. Offer products for sale as an Amazon seller: One of the

most well-liked ways to make money on Amazon is to offer products for sale as an Amazon seller. To offer products to customers directly through Amazon's marketplace, you can register as an Amazon seller.

2. Affiliate marketing: By enrolling in the Amazon Associates program, you can promote products from Amazon on your blog, website, or social media accounts. If someone uses your affiliate link to buy something, you get paid.

3. Create e-books and sell them: To create and market e-books, you can use Amazon's Kindle Direct Publishing service.

4. Print-on-demand goods: With Amazon's Merch by Amazon program, you can create and market t-shirts, mugs, and other items with your own unique designs.

5. Offer homemade goods for sale: You can offer handmade goods for sale on Amazon's handmade marketplace.

6. You can publish and sell audiobooks through Audible, a service owned by Amazon.

7. Fulfillment by Amazon (FBA): This service allows you to store and ship your products to customers through Amazon, which can help you save time and money on fulfillment.

8. Amazon Mechanical Turk: The Amazon Mechanical Turk website enables you to complete surveys or small assignments.

9. Trade-In program on Amazon: You can sell used goods using this program.

10. Amazon Flex: Anyone can work as a delivery driver through the Flex program from Amazon.

11. These are only a few of the many ways you may earn money on Amazon.

12. Choose the jobs that best fit your skills and interests to maximize your earning potential.

Alibaba

Alibaba is a multinational Chinese technology company with

expertise in e-commerce, retail, internet and technology. It was developed in 1999 by Jack Ma in Hangzhou, China. Initially, the company served as a business-to-business (B2B) marketplace enabling Chinese manufacturers to sell their goods to foreign companies. Following its early success, Taobao, a consumer-to-consumer (C2C) website, was introduced in 2003. eBay and Amazon were quickly surpassed by Taobao to become the biggest online marketplace in China. In 2005, Alibaba launched Alipay, an online payment system that swiftly grew to be a crucial part of the business' ecosystem by enabling transactions between its various platforms. When Alibaba went public on the New York Stock Exchange in 2014, it raised $25 billion, making it the largest initial public offering (IPO) in history at the time. The business continued to expand swiftly, buying other companies, funding startups, and starting new initiatives. Some of Alibaba's current ventures include Taobao, Tmall, Alibaba Cloud, Cainiao, and Ant Group (formerly Ant Financial). The company has developed into one of the biggest e-commerce giants in the world, with a market worth of more than $500 billion.

Alibaba's goods and services

Alibaba is a sizable online marketplace that connects buyers and sellers from across the globe. The company offers a range of goods and services, such as:

1. Consumer products: Alibaba offers a large selection of consumer goods, such as clothing, electronics, furniture, home appliances, and toys.
2. Industrial goods: The company offers a broad range of industrial goods, including equipment, tools, hardware, and building materials.
3. Alibaba offers wholesale goods in a range of industries, including fashion, cosmetics, sports, and home & garden.
4. Alibaba offers a range of commercial services, such as cloud computing, web hosting, and online advertising.
5. Logistics and delivery: The company offers warehousing,

customs clearance, and shipping as examples of the logistics and delivery services it offers to its clients.

6. Alibaba offers a variety of financial services, including payment processing, loans, and insurance.
7. Digital media and entertainment: Alibaba provides digital media and entertainment services like as video streaming and music streaming.
8. These are only a handful of Alibaba's goods and services. To suit the demands of its clients, the organization is constantly extending its services.

Methods for earning on alibaba

1. Product selling: Alibaba is a major online marketplace where you may sell your items. You may register as a seller and post your items for sale. You will be responsible for shipping the items to the customer, and Alibaba will charge a commission on the transaction.
2. Dropshipping: Alibaba also provides dropshipping services, allowing you to sell items without having to keep inventories. When a consumer purchases a product from your website, you may buy it from Alibaba and have it transported straight to the customer.
3. Alibaba has an affiliate program through which you may advertise their items on your website or social media platforms. All sales made through your affiliate link will earn you a commission.
4. Alibaba provides a variety of commercial services, including internet advertising, web hosting, and cloud computing. Offering these services to businesses can make you money.
5. Investing: Alibaba is a publicly listed corporation whose shares may be purchased through a brokerage account. Profits can be made if the stock price rises.
6. It's vital to realize that generating money on Alibaba takes time and planning. You'll need to do market research, find the best items or services to sell, and create a marketing

strategy to attract clients.

eBay

eBay is a global e-commerce firm based in the United States that operates an online auction and shopping website. Here's a quick look at eBay's history: Pierre Omidyar established eBay in San Jose, California in September 1995. The site, formerly known as AuctionWeb, was designed to assist Omidyar's girlfriend, who collected Pez candy dispensers, in finding other collectors online. By 1996, eBay had over 250,000 registered members and was producing millions of dollars in transactions. eBay went public in 1998, raising $63 million in its first public offering (IPO). eBay launched its worldwide site the same year, allowing people from all over the world to buy and sell on the marketplace. During the next decade, eBay grew by acquiring firms like PayPal (an online payment system), Skype (a communication platform), and StubHub (a ticket resale website). eBay experienced rising competition from other e-commerce platforms, such as Amazon, in the early 2000s. To remain competitive, eBay began to emphasize fixed-price transactions rather than auctions. eBay broke out PayPal into a separate publicly listed corporation in 2015, and the firm still operates as a worldwide online platform for consumers and sellers today.

eBay's goods and services

1. Fashion: Clothes, shoes, accessories, jewelry, watches, and so on.
2. Electronics: Including mobile phones, laptops, desktop computers, tablets, cameras, game consoles, and so on.
3. Furniture: Home décor, kitchen and dining goods, bedding, bath, and so forth.
4. Automobiles: Motorbikes, boats, parts and accessories, and so forth.
5. Collectibles: Including art, antiques, coins, stamps, mementos, and so on.
6. Sports goods: Including fitness equipment, outdoor sports

equipment, and team sports equipment, among other things.

7. Toys & Hobbies: Including things like action figures, dolls, educational toys, board games, puzzles, and so on.
8. Commercial and industrial supplies: Including office equipment, tools, and industrial supplies.
9. Personal care goods: Cosmetics, scents, vitamins, and so forth.
10. Musical instruments: Including guitars, keyboards, drums, and DJ equipment.

These are just a few examples of the various things available on eBay. eBay has a huge assortment of products from all over the world, making it an excellent location to find unusual and difficult-to-find things.

Methods for earning on ebay

1. Selling goods: You may sell stuff that you no longer need or desire, or you can buy products in bulk and resell them on eBay for a profit.
2. Dropshipping: Is the practice of putting things for sale on eBay without actually owning the inventory. When a customer puts an order, you instead buy the item from a supplier who sends it straight to the customer.
3. Arbitrage: is the practice of purchasing products on eBay or other online marketplaces and reselling them at a higher price on eBay.
4. Affiliate marketing allows you to make money by advertising eBay items and receiving a fee on purchases made via your unique affiliate link.
5. Establishing an eBay store: You may create an eBay store to exhibit your items and grow a following.

CHAPTER 7

MAKE EXTRA DOLLARS FROM COMPANIES THAT OFFER ONLINE TUTORING AND EXAM PREPARATION

General overview: Online teachers are in high demand in today's fast-paced educational environment. Offering your expertise online as a teacher or tutor could enable you to generate extra income or perhaps a full-time employment from the comfort of your home. While promoting your business online, you can offer training services offline as well. Your clients can get in touch with you by voice chat, email, MSN, or phone. Additionally, they are able to email you attachments of their projects, essays, and assignments for assessment and you will be able to assist them as needed. Your primary source of revenue will be your hourly wage. You'll need tutoring experience or expertise in a subject like calculus that often calls for a tutor. Basic Web publishing skills are necessary because you must be able to maintain your company's website and communicate clearly and succinctly.

Here are some online tutoring platforms that you can key in to make money:

Chegg Tutors

Introduction to chegg Tutors: A platform for online tutoring called Chegg Tutors links students with tutors who specialize in different topic areas. Aayush Phumbhra, Osman Rashid, and Josh Carlson established the business in 2001 as Chegg Inc., a company that rented out textbooks. Renting textbooks instead of buying them outright was intended to give students a more cost-effective option to get the materials they need. Online tutoring, test preparation, and other educational materials have been added to the company's services over the years. InstaEDU, an online tutoring platform, was purchased by the business in 2014, and its technology was incorporated into its own platform, which was later renamed Chegg Tutors. Students get access to a sizable pool of subject-specific tutors through Chegg Tutors. Through the platform's virtual whiteboard, messaging feature, and audio/video chat, students can communicate with tutors. Students can plan sessions, monitor their progress, and receive comments on their work using the platform's other functions. Chegg Tutors is becoming a well-liked choice for students looking for online tutoring services. The platform provides access to a variety of tutors, flexible scheduling, and reasonable fees. Other educational services, such test preparation and textbook solutions, have been added to the company's list of services.

How to join Chegg tutors and earn

1. Create a Chegg Tutors account: By going to the website at https://www.chegg.com/tutors/ and selecting "Become a tutor." Your name, email address, and password must be entered while creating an account, among other personal data.

2. Complete your profile: After creating an account, you will be prompted to complete your profile. Information on your educational background, professional background, and the subjects you intend to teach are all included. To make your profile stand out, be sure to include as much information as you can.

3. Pass the subject test: Before beginning tuition, Chegg Tutors needs all tutors to pass a subject test. The purpose of the subject test is to gauge your level of knowledge and proficiency in the subject you want to teach.

4. Apply for tutoring positions: After passing the subject exam, you can begin applying for tutoring positions on the Chegg Tutors website. Subject, grade level, and geographical search options are available for tutoring positions.

5. Scheduling tutoring sessions: If you are recruited as a tutor,

you will be required to meet with the student on a specific date and time. With the help of Chegg Tutors, you can conduct the tutoring session in an online classroom.

6.   Receive payment: Chegg Tutors pays its tutors once each week. Payment will be made for the tutoring sessions you delivered the previous week. Employing PayPal or direct deposit, Chegg Tutors compensates its tutors.

To sum up, in order to become a teacher on Chegg Tutors, you must first register an account, complete your profile, pass the subject test, apply for tutoring positions, set up tutoring sessions, and collect payment for your work. There are other platforms own by chegg they are TutorMe (TutorMe - http://tutorme.com/) and TeachMeNow (http://teachmenow.com/) You can also check their website for more opportunities to earn.

COURSE HERO

American education technology company Course Hero is situated in Redwood City, California, and operates an online learning platform that students can utilize for a fee in order to obtain course-specific study materials. To use the platform, students must subscribe. By helping students from all around the world with their knowledge and abilities, tutors on Course Hero can make up to $1,500 per month. The amount that each tutor will really be paid will vary depending on factors including how many questions they have answered, how difficult they were to answer, what they were about, and how well they were answered.

Step by step guide on how to use course hero

1. Register an account at https://www.coursehero.com/login/: You must first register an account in order to utilize Course Hero. To sign up, you can do so using your email address, Facebook account, or Google account.
2. After signing up, look through Course Hero's library of study materials, which includes study guides, lecture notes, and practice examinations. You can either conduct a

topic-specific search or browse by category.

3. Upload content: If you wish to share your study materials with others, you can do so on Course Hero. You will receive unlocks for each document you upload, which you can use to unlock further platform docs.

4. Unlock content: In order to access some Course Hero study materials, you'll need to use unlocks. You can submit your own study materials or buy them from the platform to get unlocks.

5. Question-and-answer session: Hero also features a Q&A part where students can pose and receive responses to inquiries on the relevant courses. By posing and responding to questions, unlocks can be acquired.

6. Earn incentives: Course Hero provides a rewards system that allows you to earn free unlocks, scholarships, and other benefits.

7. Take into account the subscription: Even if Course Hero offers a lot of content for free, some of it can be protected by a paywall. If you want access to infinite unlocks and other features think about purchasing a membership.

Course Hero might be a useful complement to a student's curriculum and general study materials. You can be rewarded for uploading study materials, answering questions, and inviting others to use the platform.

Preply

Introduction to preply: Preply began by concentrating primarily on providing instruction in the English language, but it has now grown to provide tutoring in over 50 different languages, including Spanish, French, German, Chinese, and Arabic. Students can find private tutors from all over the world using the online language learning platform Preply. Entrepreneur Kirill Bigai of Ukraine started it in 2012 after having trouble finding a language tutor for himself. Every lesson given on Preply's platform is subject to a commission fee as part of its business strategy.

It also provides other features like session scheduling, payment processing, and progress tracking.

How to become a tutor at Preply

1. Sign up: By entering your personal data and login credentials, create an account on Preply at http://preply.com/

2. Create your profile: Include pertinent details about your teaching experience, credentials, and abilities in your profile.

3. Select the topics that best suit your schedule: Choose the topics you want to teach, then indicate your availability.

4. Pass the interview: Preply will speak with you in an interview to evaluate your language and teaching abilities.

5. Define your rates: Set hourly rates for each subject that you teach.

6. begin training: You can begin instructing pupils and making money once you've been given the go-ahead.

Make sure your profile is thorough and well-written, highlight your teaching experience and credentials, and be well-prepared for the interview to maximize your chances of being accepted.

1. Skooli - http://www.skooli.com/
2. Wyzant - http://www.wyzant.com/
3. Tutorful - http://tutorful.co.uk/
4. Varsity Tutors - http://www.varsitytutors.com/
5. LearnPick - http://www.learnpick.com/
6. HeyTutor - http://heytutor.com/

Summarily; there are many opportunities make dollars in companies that run online tutoring and exams preparation, the ones we discussed above were sampled out for the purpose of educating you about the opportunities therein. I provided some more websites for you to also search more opportunities.

CHAPTER 8

MARKING MONEY FROM CROWD SOURCING

Introduction

Crowdsourcing is the gathering of information, views, or work from a large number of individuals, typically over the Internet. Paid crowdsourcing is a type of crowdsourcing where individuals are compensated for contributing their time, skills, or resources to a particular project or task. It is a way for businesses or organizations to tap into a diverse pool of talent and expertise without hiring full-time employees. Paid crowdsourcing is typically facilitated through online platforms, which connect businesses with a global network of individuals who are willing to provide their services. These platforms offer a wide range of tasks, such as data entry, market research, content creation, and product testing. Participants can choose to work on projects that match their skills and interests, and are usually paid a fee for their work. One of the most common forms of paid crowdsourcing is microtasking, which involves breaking down a larger project into small, discrete tasks that can be completed quickly and easily by individuals in the crowd. Microtasks can include things like image tagging, transcription, or data entry. Participants can complete these tasks in their spare time, and are paid for each task they successfully complete. Paid crowdsourcing has become increasingly popular in recent years as a way for businesses to access talent from around the world, and for individuals to earn money or support causes they care about.

TOP 15 LEGIT CROWDSOURCING COMPANIES THAT ARE EASY TO JOIN

1. **Amazon Mechanical Turk**: This is one of the largest and most popular crowdsourcing platforms that allows individuals to complete simple tasks for pay. It's easy to sign up and start working.

2. **Clickworker**: Clickworker is another reputable crowdsourcing platform that offers a wide range of microtasks. Signing up is straightforward and you can start earning money right away.

3. **Swagbucks**: Swagbucks is a popular platform that offers various ways to earn money, including completing surveys, watching videos, and playing games. Signing up is free and straightforward.

4. **Appen**: Appen is a crowdsourcing platform that offers a variety of work-from-home opportunities such as data annotation, speech recognition, and search relevance evaluation. It's easy to join and they provide clear instructions on how to complete tasks.

5. **Prolific**: Prolific is a platform that offers paid surveys to researchers and participants. It's easy to sign up and start earning money by completing surveys on various topics.

6. **Scribie**: Scribie is a transcription platform that offers work-at-home opportunities for transcribers. Signing up is easy and you can start working right away.

7. **UserTesting**: UserTesting is a platform that pays you to test websites and apps. Signing up is straightforward and you can start earning money immediately.

8. **Respondent**: Respondent is a platform that offers paid research studies to participants. It's easy to join and you can start earning money by participating in studies that match your profile.

9. **Clicks Research**: Clicks Research is a platform that pays you to complete online surveys. Signing up is free and you can start earning money right away.

10. **CrowdFlower**: CrowdFlower is a crowdsourcing platform that offers various microtasks to individuals. Signing up is easy and you can start earning money by completing simple tasks.

11. **TranscribeMe**: TranscribeMe is a transcription platform that pays individuals to transcribe audio and video files. Signing up is easy and you can start working right away.

12. **OneSpace**: OneSpace is a platform that offers a variety of work-from-home opportunities such as data entry, transcription, and writing. It's easy to join and they provide clear instructions on how to complete tasks.
13. **Spare5**: Spare5 is a platform that pays you to complete simple tasks such as image tagging and content moderation. Signing up is easy and you can start earning money right away.
14. **Remotasks**: Remotasks is a platform that offers various microtasks such as image annotation, transcription, and data categorization. Signing up is easy and you can start earning money by completing tasks.
15. **Lionbridge**: Lionbridge is a platform that offers a variety of work-from-home opportunities such as translation, transcription, and data entry. It's easy to join and they provide clear instructions on how to complete tasks.

SELECTED AND DISCUSSED LEGIT CROWDSOURCING COMPANIES

Amazon mechanical Turk step by step

Thanks to Amazon Mechanical Turk (MTurk), a crowdsourcing marketplace that made it simpler for people and organizations to outsource their processes and duties to a distributed workforce that can complete these activities digitally. This might range from performing straightforward data validation and research to more ethereal jobs like taking part in surveys, content moderation, and more. Utilizing the collective intelligence, expertise, and insights of a global workforce through MTurk enables businesses to accelerate machine learning development, improve data collection and analysis, and streamline business processes. Even though technology is constantly evolving, there are still many tasks that humans perform much more efficiently than computers, such as content moderation, data duplication, and research. Such duties have typically been left undone or completed by engaging a sizable temporary staff, which is time-consuming, costly, and challenging to scale. A physical, time-consuming activity can be divided into smaller, more manageable tasks using crowdsourcing, which is sometimes known as "microtasking," and then carried out by dispersed employees online. At Amazon the job is often described as human intelligence task (HIT) workers are to complete a given HIT and then requesters approve it before such task is paid.

Requesters have tasks they need to be completed   MTurk Marketplace   Workers want to earn money and work on interesting tasks

(Image sourced from https://www.mturk.com/)

The image above shows how workers and requesters meet at MTurk marketplace. While requesters bring in their tasks they needed to be completed, workers want to earn money by working on the interesting tasks. In general, Amazon Mechanical Turk is a platform that links requesters with individuals who need modest, straightforward jobs done for payment. It's a convenient and open method for employees to make money online, and it's an economical option for companies to outsource labor.

HOW TO SIGN UP STEP BT STEP

1. Go to the Amazon Mechanical Turk website: The first step is to go to the Amazon Mechanical Turk website. You can do this by typing "www.mturk.com" into your web browser or by clicking on this link: https://www.mturk.com/.

2. Click on the "Worker" button: Once you are on the Amazon Mechanical Turk homepage, you will see a button in the top right-hand corner that says "Worker". Click on this button.

3. Click on the "Create an Account" button: On the next page, you will see a blue button labeled "Create an Account". Click on this button.

4. Fill out your information: On the registration page, you will be asked to fill out your personal information, such as your name, email address, and password. You will also be asked to agree to the terms of service and privacy policy. After you have filled out the information, click on the "Create Account" button.

5. Confirm your email address: After you have created your account, Amazon Mechanical Turk will send you an email to confirm your email address. Check your email and click on the link in the email to confirm your account.

6. Complete your profile: Once you have confirmed your email address, you will be asked to complete your profile. You will need to provide additional information, such as your address and payment information. You will also need to complete a tax form so that Amazon Mechanical Turk can properly report your earnings to the IRS.

7. Start working: After you have completed your profile, you can start working on tasks on Amazon Mechanical Turk. You can browse available tasks by clicking on the "Find HITs" button on the top of the page. When you find a task you want to work on, click on the task title to see the details and instructions.

HOW MTurk WORKS STEP BY STEP

1. Requesters create HITs: Requesters create HITs (Human Intelligence Tasks) and post them on the Amazon Mechanical Turk platform. HITs can be simple tasks like surveys, data entry, image tagging, or more complex tasks like transcription and data analysis.

2. Workers search for HITs: Workers browse available HITs on the platform and choose the ones they want to complete. They can filter HITs by category, pay rate, and other factors.

3. Workers complete HITs: Workers complete the selected HITs according to the instructions provided by the requester. They must complete the tasks accurately and submit them within the specified time frame.

4. Requesters approve or reject HITs: Once workers submit their completed HITs, the requester reviews them and approves or rejects them. If a HIT is rejected, the worker won't receive payment for that task.

5. Workers receive payment: Once the requester approves a completed HIT, the worker receives payment for their work. The

payment amount depends on the complexity of the task and the requester's pay rate.

6. Workers can build a reputation: Workers can build a reputation on the platform by completing tasks accurately and on time. This can lead to more work opportunities in the future.

7. Requesters can provide bonuses: Requesters can provide bonuses to workers who complete tasks exceptionally well. This can encourage workers to do their best and improve their reputation on the platform.

FREQUENTLY ASKED QUESTIONS ABOUT MTurk AND ANSWERS

1.   What is Amazon Mechanical Turk? Amazon Mechanical Turk is an online platform that allows requesters to post small, simple tasks called HITs (Human Intelligence Tasks) for workers to complete for pay.

2.   Who can work on Amazon Mechanical Turk? Anyone who is over 18 years old and has an Amazon account can work on Amazon Mechanical Turk.

3.   How much can I earn on Amazon Mechanical Turk? The pay for HITs on Amazon Mechanical Turk can vary widely, depending on the complexity of the task and the requester's pay rate. Some HITs may pay only a few cents, while others may pay several dollars.

4.   How do I get paid on Amazon Mechanical Turk? You can receive payments for your completed HITs via Amazon Payments. You can then transfer your earnings to your bank account or use them to make purchases on Amazon.

5.   How do I find HITs to work on? You can browse available HITs on the Amazon Mechanical Turk platform and filter them by category, pay rate, and other factors. You can also set up alerts for new HITs in your preferred categories.

6.   How do I know if a requester is trustworthy? Amazon Mechanical Turk has a system for requester ratings and reviews, so you can check the ratings and reviews of a requester before you decide to work on their HITs. You can also check the requester's approval and rejection rates.

7.   Can I work on Amazon Mechanical Turk full-time? While some workers do work on Amazon Mechanical Turk full-time, the platform is better suited for part-time or supplemental work. The availability and pay rates of HITs can fluctuate, so it may not be reliable as a full-time source of income.

8. What happens if a requester rejects my work? If a requester rejects your work, you won't receive payment for that HIT. However, you can try to contact the requester and ask for feedback on why your work was rejected, or dispute the rejection if you believe it was unwarranted.

9. Can I work on Amazon Mechanical Turk from any location? Yes, you can work on Amazon Mechanical Turk from anywhere in the world, as long as you have an Amazon account and a valid payment method.

10. Is Amazon Mechanical Turk a scam? No, Amazon Mechanical Turk is a legitimate platform for workers to complete tasks for pay. However, as with any online platform, there may be scammers who try to take advantage of workers, so it's important to be cautious and do your research before accepting HITs from unfamiliar requesters.

11. How do I add an account to get paid on Amazon Mechanical Turk? To add an account to get paid on Amazon Mechanical Turk, you need to set up an Amazon Payments account. You can do this by going to the Amazon Payments website and following the instructions to create an account.

12. What payment methods are available on Amazon Mechanical Turk? The payment methods available on Amazon Mechanical Turk depend on the country you are in. In the United States, you can receive payments via direct deposit, Amazon gift card, or check. In other countries, payment options may include bank transfer, prepaid debit card, or other options.

13. How long does it take to get paid on Amazon Mechanical Turk? The time it takes to get paid on Amazon Mechanical Turk depends on several factors, including the payment method you choose and the payment schedule of the requester. Some requesters pay immediately upon completion of a HIT, while others may take several days or weeks to approve and pay for completed work. Once payment is approved, it may take an additional few days for the payment to be processed and transferred to your account.

14. How do I change my payment method on Amazon Mechanical Turk? To change your payment method on Amazon Mechanical Turk, you need to go to your Amazon Payments account and update your payment settings. You can choose a new payment method or update your bank account or debit card information.

15. Can I receive payments in a different currency on Amazon Mechanical Turk? Yes, you can receive payments in a different currency on Amazon Mechanical Turk. However, you may be subject

to currency conversion fees or exchange rates that could affect the amount of payment you receive. It's important to check with your payment provider or bank to understand the fees and exchange rates associated with receiving payments in a different currency.

16. How long does it take to get a completed HIT approved for MTurk? Amazon Mechanical Turk cannot predict when they will be accepted. After you submit your Human Intelligence Tasks (HITs), Requesters have 30 days to decide whether to approve your work and pay you or not. It is up to you to decide whether to accept or reject HITs, and Visit the

17. How much money is paid by Amazon Mechanical Turk? According to a platform analysis published in 2018, of the 3.8 million examined jobs completed by 2676 individuals, an average hourly salary for these workers was roughly $2. While only 4% of workers received pay above $7.25 per hour.

18. How do I add a bank account to Amazon Mturk? Visit https://payments.amazon.com and log in. Navigate to "Edit My Account Setting" in your Payments account. "Add bank account" should be clicked. Give your account information, including your bank account holder name, routing number, account number, and account type (individual or business checking account).

19. Can money earned from MTurk be withdrawn at any time? You can deposit or withdraw funds from your Mechanical Turk account at any time using the Requester website (http://requester.mturk.amazon.com/)

ABOUT THE AUTHOR

Jd Bigwama

JD Bigwama is a multi-talented individual born on 24th May 1988 in Fadama Jankasa Village, Lere LGA, Kaduna State, Nigeria. He received his primary education at LEA Primary School Jankasa and his JSS1-3 education at Government Junior Secondary School Maigamoh. JD then proceeded to Government Technical College Soba, where he completed his SS1-3 education. In 2010, JD enrolled at Ahmadu Bello University, Zaria, where he studied Electrical and Computer Engineering until 2015. After  graduation, he started working as a teacher in a secondary school in Kano, Nigeria, while still practicing his engineering profession. JD married his beautiful wife, Anthonia Yakubu, in 2022, and they have been happily married since then. Apart from his engineering and teaching professions, JD is also interested in writing and researching. He is particularly keen on discovering ways to make extra money and improve his financial status. JD Bigwama is an inspiring individual who embodies hard work and determination. He is a role model to many, and his achievements are a testament to his dedication and commitment to excellence.

www.ingramcontent.com/pod-product-compliance
Lightning Source LLC
Chambersburg PA
CBHW070453220526
45466CB00004B/1815